MELANCHOLIC HOPE
POEMS ON BREAKING AND MENDING

Hope Pratt

BookLeaf
Publishing
India | USA | UK

Melancholic Hope

© 2021 Hope Pratt

Presentation by *BookLeaf Publishing*

Web: www.bookleafpub.com

E-mail: info@bookleafpub.com

ISBN: 9789358361582

First edition 2021

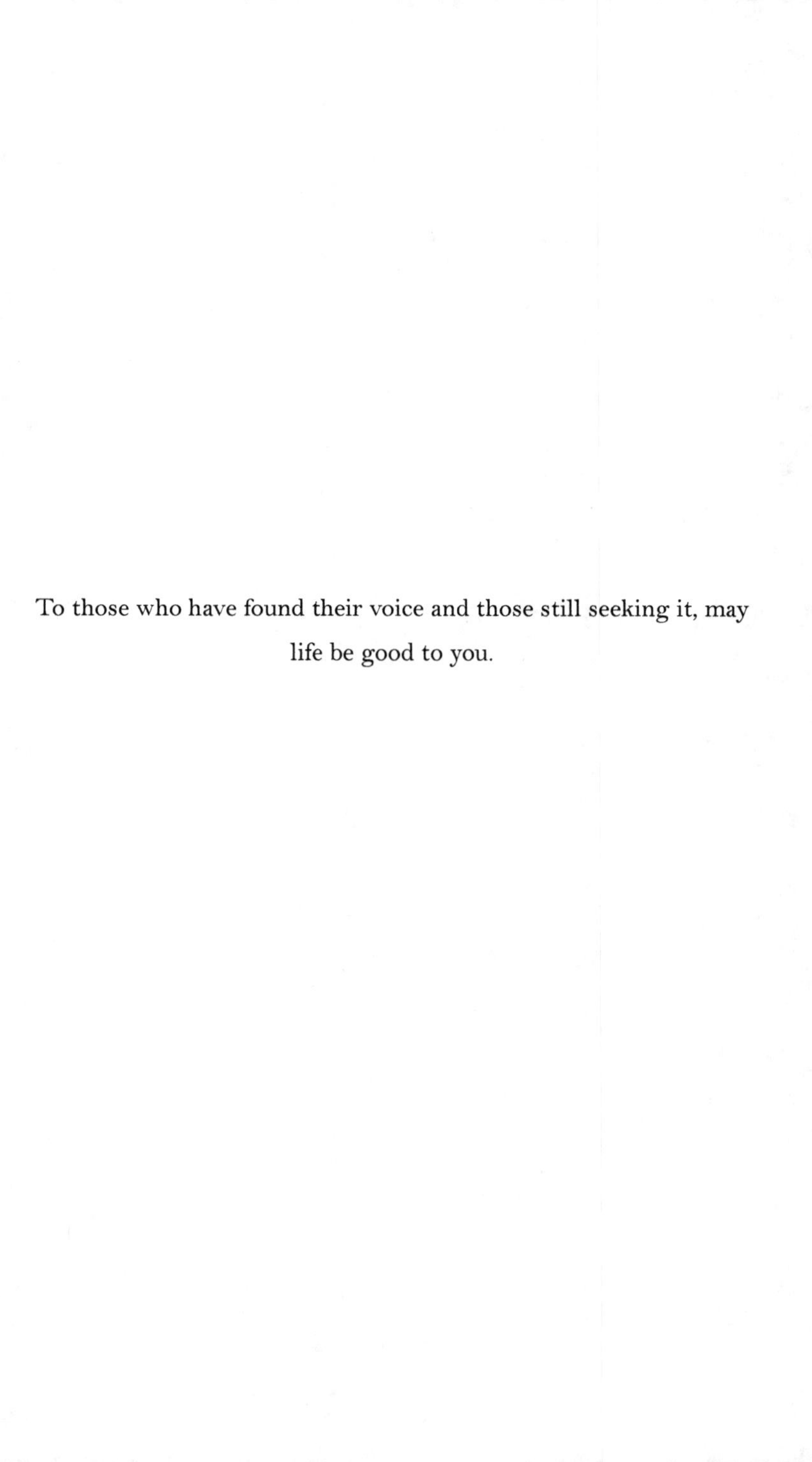

To those who have found their voice and those still seeking it, may life be good to you.

ACKNOWLEDGEMENTS

I would like to begin by thanking my mum Stephanie, my dad Lee, and my sister Kaylyn for all the love they have given me over the years. I would also like to thank my friends, Bek Grimmond, Emily Shilling, Hannah Bailey, Jess Murphy, Jasmine Brading, Dana Bewick, Sarah Tingle, Hannah Guez, Caity Riley, and Elizabeth Laughton; you all have been people who have encouraged me, and for that I say thank you. To my high school teachers, Mrs Key, Ms Young, Ms Lewis, Mrs Jelfs, and Mrs Fowler, thank you for believing in me, even when I couldn't myself. And finally, to my girlfriend Lauren; you are kind and wonderful, thank you for being in my life.

PREFACE

I usually write in prose, but some emotions require the poetic. I have always loved the poetry of John Keats and Margret Atwood and how they so easily describe what it means to love, to grieve, to be sad. Writing connects people and poetry can so wonderfully express the inexpressible. Metaphor and simile connect complexity to simplicity and lets empathy breathe. So, this book is the result of that. I hope you enjoy it, even if it's just to laugh at its melodrama. But here it is, poems on being queer, on love, on religion, on breaking and on mending. If it speaks to you, I'm glad for that, if it doesn't, I hope you find the words that express what you feel.

DAY 1

ON LOVE NO. 1

I crave a deeper love
An "I'll do anything for you" love
A "good night sweetheart" love
The type of love that's deeper than seas and stronger than their
waves

I want the sort of love that sings
The love that will lean over to you at the movies and say, "I know
that guy from somewhere"
The type that holds your hand in public, even when everyone is
watching
The form of love that whispers instead of shouts
The one that leaves you feeling it all

I want a sweeter kind of love
A "you look beautiful today and everyday" love
A "kiss me softly" love
A "hold me tight and love me long time" type that lingers on

Something soft and sweet and slow
Something patient
Something steady

DAY 2

ON NAMES AND THEIR OWNERS

It's getting harder for me to say your name again, but I think that's
a good thing.
For all the times I practiced it and mulled it over in my head, it gets
caught in my throat now.
It used to roll more easily off my tongue but today, I stumble and
stammer and stutter over it.
I can't help but miss its difficulty, how it kept me on my toes, how it
would so forcefully demand to be pronounced and said aloud.
It was a name worth time and concentration and battles with one's
own articulation.
But now, I'm starting to realise there is more comfort in
uncomplicated names, ones you don't have to practice and please
with every vowel.
Ones that are kinder and more patient when I fumble it.
Ones that will say my own name with affection and quiet fervour.
Ones that will listen and hear and respond in clemency.
Still, with no strings attached, I can't help mourning the loss of a
name as harsh as yours.

DAY 3

THE TRAVELLER, ABANDONED

I feel as though I am wasting away to skin and bones
I will be some husk of a thing, dry and barren in these Badlands
I will wait for some Samaritan to come along and carry me to the
nearest homestead, where I can drink and eat my fill

Otherwise, perhaps I could use my bones to build a priest's fire
Make it glow and spark, be a martyr for the hopeful
Suffer for their postulating as they cry, "look at the fire I've built
from dead bones!"
And I will sit in their burning flames, consumed

Yet, somewhere in the depths of these sallow cheeks, in this sunken
sternum, there is a flicker of esprit still to be found
So maybe I could muster my last breaths to drag my body across
the desert to some Oasis or Well
Then bring myself to my feet to drink and wash
To clean my wounds, to cleanse my soul
And then perhaps I can wander again through the wilderness,
searching for the land of milk and honey

DAY 4

NEW LOVE

I can feel a space in my heart being filled by you
You are slow and cautious, but I can feel you there
I think this is a kinder way to love someone
As thrilling the elation to rush into another's life is, it's messy and
brutal
Nothing compares to a slow burn
A simmering heat, that warms gradually and before you know it,
you're ablaze
Its heat is patient in waiting for permission and reciprocity
It is careful with your heart and gentle holding it
Instead of flames and spitting embers, it is enduring coals
Smouldering and glowing

DAY 5

SAVIOUR COMPLEX

My dear, let me bind up your wounds for you and cover your scars
Let me wrap your scrapes in cotton bandages and dry your eyes
with linen kerchiefs

Darling, I would soothe every headache and ease every sprain
I'd bring pillows and blankets, and aspirin for your head

Lovely, I could spend hours mending your broken heart even if it
meant using pieces of mine
I'd rather be empty than have you be hollow

Every scraped knee
Every black eye
Every bloody nose
I would come to make sure the blood didn't stain the carpet
I would get the ice pack from the freezer and the plasters from the
cupboard
I would hold you close, kiss it all better

DAY 6

ON LOVE NO. 2

Love is not violent
It is soft and unassuming
It is seeing the little things and noticing when they cut their hair
It is remembering dates, and birthdays, and how they like their
eggs in the morning
It is also being bold
Confessing your affections without fear of consequence

Love is not cruel
It doesn't not torment, or play games, or hit or slap
It is your hand clasped in mine
It is my head rested on your shoulder
Your eyes looking into mine

Love is not harsh words or violent phrases flung at one another in
desperation
It is sweet nothings
It is poems and letters
It is "can I get you anything?" or "how was your day?"

Love is not hurt
It is balm to old wounds
It is a mighty tenderness placed before another

DAY 7

A PSALMIST IN A STORM

His words are a roar of thunder
His commands the pelting rains that hit my back in bullets
Adrift in waters his judgement abounds
All I can see are the blackening clouds and shocks of lightning
overhead
It is with pure praise I call out to you "Abba, father!"
It is with plain humility I ask for grace
But perhaps the waves are merciful in their terror
Perhaps they are to drown me in your love and have me wash upon
the shore anew

His voice is the calming seas
His hand the clearing blue skies
As I follow the briny deep, I'm still in your keep
You call me out on these waters, oh me of little faith
I step on the expanse of the sea and plunge into the cold
As I sink, I hear the currents sing your glory and the sand bare
your majesty
As I break the surface, birds call your name
A nautical hymn for your adoration

DAY 8

THE LOVE OF THE DAMNED

I would burn for you
I would catch a light and smoulder to ash
I would toss my body into hell fire to hold your hand
To kiss you I would pay penance a thousand times over
To hug your body to mine I would take nine lashes from the rod
To taste you I would waste away in Sheol
I would trade Eden for Gehenna

But…

I would live for you
I would run from flames into your arms
I would break chains to have you hold my face to yours
To wake in your embrace, I relinquish hesitation
To have you brush your lips to my neck I throw away my shame
To have you clasp my waist I would toss aside cowardice with
reckless abandon
I would be fully me and nothing less

DAY 9

THE LAMB & THE LION

Everything is bleak and damp in the woods.
There is nothing but cold.
It cuts to the bone, and I am left chilled.

The edge of the forest is full of thorns and tall in its threatening.
A white lamb approaches and grazes my leg.
As I turn, she looks up at me in longing, in pleading.
For some adventure, some journey to the beyond?
So, I can do nothing else but gather her in my arms and carry her
with me.

The trees move in close and tower above us.
They whisper and taunt, wailing their secrets.
The branches scrape and scratch me, they catch in the Lamb's coat
as she bleats.
I break through the brambles, cut and scraped.
I see blood flecks her fleece and I apologise,
I sincerely apologise as I pick the wood from her wool.

As we trod on the beaten path the dark consumes us.
All that can be seen are the stars and the moon.
They break through the canopy making speckled patterns on the
path.
Then a low groan breaks from the trees.

We stop, bloody lamb and bloody human.
Behind the fallen trunk ahead emerges the gold of a Lion.
Furry and passion ripples from his throat,
Power and vigour are his form.
Polite and stern he asks to join us on our walk.
I say yes, maybe from fear, maybe from hope, and we carry on.

When I get tired the Lion offers me his back.
I lay comfortably in his mane with the Lamb singing a song.
Sometimes I look up to the stars and I weep from their beauty.
The moon comforts me by her light.
And then I drift off to sleep.

Soon I am on my blistered feet again limping to the clearing.
The dawn is beginning to break, and I am aching.
I am hurting.
I am battered and bruised.
I am in rags.
I am collapsed to my knees.
But the Lion lets me lean into is mane again.
The Lamb sings her song again.
So, I sleep again as the warm sun welcomes us.

DAY 10

THE FATHER

I cried the day you left
That night I beat my chest wailing your name
I tore my clothes screaming after you

"My son, my son!"

If it hadn't been for my weak knees
I would have run after you
Clutching the hem of your shirt I would have begged you to stay
But I didn't
You would have left anyway

I have spent my days
My weeks
My months
My years
Sitting in the paddocks
Watching the rolling hills of green
With hope you may come home
With hope you may stay

One day I thought I saw you at the marketplace
It was Sunday and you were picking pears and pomegranates
I called out

"My son, my dear boy!"

In response was only the low bustle of the streets

I began waiting on the road instead
There was better chance of you coming home that way
I waited there three days
And when I saw you, I thought it was a dream
But I picked up my feet anyway
I ran with my frail knees
Arms outstretched, abandoned in promise

When I reached you, I wept
In joy and grief
I couldn't help but hold you close and whisper

"My son, my child."

"For this son of mine was dead and he is alive; he was lost and is found."
– Luke 15:24 (NIV)

DAY 11
YOUR NAME TO ME

What should I call you?
When we hold hands in the church parking lot
Is 'my love' too much?
Is 'sweetheart' too quiet
I would shout it if you wanted
I would whisper it too
And what about when we kiss at the movies?
Should I whisper to you 'my darling'?
Or should I say 'I love you dearly' with my eyes?
Whether silent or hushed I hope you hear it
I hope you carry that knowledge in your heart

I think a picture of us would look nice on my desk at work
That way when I get bored and people ask, "Who is she?"
I can say, 'the one who has my heart. The one who dwells in my
soul'
And whether they are puzzled or give withering stares
I would say it with my whole chest
I would say it over and over again

How about when I hold you at night?
When we are skin to skin
When we're sweaty body on sweaty body
Is 'you are beautiful' enough?
Or is there something deeper you want to hear?

It's your pick

Anyway, I want to say it
I want to say what your name is to me

DAY 12

THE SKELETON IN THE CHURCH'S CLOSET

I am the skeleton in the church's closet
Every church must have at least one
In the corner of the chapel is my wardrobe
It is a lovely dark stained oak
But it is quiet and dim most days
But that's home

Most of the time I sit and ponder my bones
I think of their dryness
Of their brittle nature
Once brilliant white
They are now a pale yellow
Blankets of dust cover them
Grime and grit have leeched into my joints
Rats have found solace in my ribs and sternum
Perhaps that's why I live in my closet
The muck has gotten to me for far too long

In the day I'm not allowed out
The Reverend says it's bad for my bones
"The sun is deceptive" he tells me
He is my only friend
Sometimes I think of going out on a Sunday morning though
I can see light leak in through the cracks of my door

I can hear the muffled voices sing
I can feel the warmth of company
I can smell burnt coffee and biscuits from the chapel kitchen
I long to taste and smell and hear and gaze on it all for real
I imagine singing out of tune in the pews
From the pulpit the Reverend would speak clear in pitch
How sweet the laughter would be heard up close?
How lovely the choir wound echo through the hall?
I wonder if they dance
I wonder if when they pray, they hold strangers' hands
Do they ever get angry?
Do they cry?
I cry, sometimes it's fun
Reverend says it our way of praying in silence
But I make a lot of noise

When night comes, I'm allowed to stretch my legs
So, I creep out of my closet, and I sit in the pews
I like the middle ones
From there you can see the alter ordained with candles and crucifix
alike
Everything is deep in night though and I wonder what it looks like
in bright day
Still the moon breaks the stained-glass windows
And I can watch the colours dance on the floor
If I'm lucky when the Reverend comes late, I can glimpse the start
of dawn
I can watch the purples fade to blue
Soon enough though he comes in and helps me back to my
cupboard

And that's where I stay
Curled in the corner, stiff and broken
Praying for my flesh to clothe my naked bones
Praying my skin is clean
It's a pity God can't hear skeletons

DAY 13

THE SWEATER

You're Tethered, to that sweater
The one full of holes, the one God knows
Needs to be thrown out
It makes you cold, feeds that winter chilling in your bones
It's not the only one you've got
So why not?
Just throw it out
Be done with that doubt
All it does is let the wind in
Yes, sometimes it's soft
But it makes you cough
And splutter
Stutter
Stumble over your words
Don't try to pretend it's comfy enough to stay
All it does is play
It toys
Destroys your mind
Don't try to say it makes you kind
After all it's just a sweater
So, take it off, I know you've glued it to your skin but please just
take it off
If not, after all it's just a sweater, right?

You let it sit in your closet now
On a pile of hidden clothing, you keep somehow
Stuff you've only worn once
Stuff you've put on back to front
Why not put some of it on?
Do it now before this moment's gone

DAY 14

WALLFLOWER

I'm a little flower, yellow and green. I sit in a wall and grow in its cracks. I've dug deep into its bricks so I can watch the buttercups in the fields. They sway and bend, I like to see their liberty. But truthfully, I long to be pulled away from my stones and into their meadows. If I could, I would dance with the lilacs and daisies. I would sing with the marigolds and tulips. Instead, I will slink into the tiles of a bathroom, to weep and fret. But eventually, I'll dry my eyes and slip out of its cold comfort. Then I'll dig my roots into the grout of the wall once again and I'll stare at my leaves and examine my petals, because looking at them wilting is better than dancing with no one.

DAY 15

GOOD OLD DAYS

The good old days will always have my heart,
Year after year they'll hold a part.
A neatly etched quarter tucked away in the past,
A little place I crawl to the days that didn't last.
They seem so much sweeter, almost like honey.
They seem so much better, a time that was, I must say, quite lovely.

I want for days long lost,
I yearn for the forests covered in moss.
The smell of chocolate chip cookies and the taste of sweet tea,
The sound of days spent by the sea.
Those little moments where I felt free,
The ones where I was most me.

I need time in my attic, when it's covered in rosemary and dust.
It seems for me nostalgia takes a form of lust.

Though many days have been filled with hurt,
And the frankness of life has always been curt.
It's the times that were best that find me crumpled on the floor.
They are the things that will bruise infinitely more.
Reading old words on paper scraps and sticky notes,
Feeling every sentence people wrote.
I play highlight reels of precious times with friends,

Hoping, praying, wishing that these relationships won't end.
For their kindness, love and care is what keeps me present.
They keep me from building too many fences.

Then there is a pang of blame,
A twinge of guilt, a jab of shame.
Perhaps I didn't cherish our moments long enough,
Perhaps my tenderness was too course, too rough.
So, I have to count my memories again in fondness,
A wishful thought to remember what bonds us.
My tears will come, yes, they will pour.
My joys and regrets kept score for score.
Yet somehow my heart will need more.
But all I have is to keep nostalgia at my core.

DAY 16

GOODBYES

Goodbyes make your heart brittle and cold over time.
With every last word spoken,
Every hug held,
And every hand waved,
Your heart hardens.
Then it crumbles,
And you are left to pick up the pieces,
Trying to glue it all back together.
It is only a hope,
That it still resembles a vague shape of what it once was,
But really it rarely does.

DAY 17

HOPE

It is a spark within me
A fire setting
A small blaze

In the dead of night, the moon
She guides me home
The stars comfort me

In the bright of day, the sparrows
They fly ahead of me
The snowdrops point to the earth

When I sink to my knees, my heart
It whispers for me to rise
But all I can do is crawl

Though that is enough
On your knees
Or on your feet
It still speaks

DAY 18

JOY

This is happiness enduring
It is optimism surviving
It is the sun shouting through the clouds "I am still here!"

It is a loved one's arms wrapped round you
It is a smile from a stranger
And puppy dog kisses

It is delphiniums, and gardenias, and marigolds in bloom
It is lemonade on hot days
It is the bliss of a tree's shade
And the beginning of spring

When the dawn breaks
And the sun sets
This is a new day and beginning

The morning light is a promise
One that I keep
One that is everlasting

DAY 19

FAITH

This is a fickle thing faith
It is weak and wavering
I know nothing but an unsteady belief

Doubt and trust go hand in hand
But often doubt leads
Faith walking humbly behind it

Do I dare trust in something so invisible as faith?
Perhaps on the worst of days
Perhaps on the happiest

Because what is faith if not accepting doubt and persisting?

DAY 20
PEACE

27

I don't know much about peace other than it can be found
It is the calming of an anxious heart
Or perhaps just a move to comfort it

It is often underestimated
It's braver
More gritty

It's both serine and a crescendo
And fosters reconciliation
It gives us forgiveness as gift

Still, it is so out of reach
So far off from my grasp
So, all I can do is sit on this precipice with you